GENEALOGY

GENEALOGY

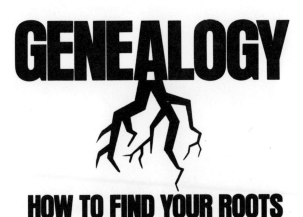

HOW TO FIND YOUR ROOTS
HENRY GILFOND

An !mpact Book
Franklin Watts / New York / London / 1978

Photographs courtesy of:
New York Public Library Picture Collection: pp.
2, 7, 8, 23, 28, 51, 62, 63; United Nations: p. 15;
Metropolitan Museum of Art: Report card: The
Elisha Whittelsey Fund, Ticket: Gift of Barrett P.
Smith, Valentine: Bella C. Landauer Collection:
p. 16; Nebraska State Historical Society: pp. 26–
27; Alaska Department of Economic Development
and Planning: p. 37; Leonard Covello (private
collection): pp. 42–43; Bernice P. Bishop Museum: p. 44; Henry Francis DuPont Winterthur
Museum: p. 47; Oregon Historical Society: pp.
58–59; Museum of the City of New York, Byron
Collection: pp. 68–69.

Library of Congress Cataloging in Publication Data

Gilfond, Henry.
    Genealogy : how to find your roots.

    (An Impact book)
    Bibliography: p.
    Includes index.
    SUMMARY: Presents step-by-step directions for
tracing lineage including routines for research and
sources of information
        1. Genealogy—Juvenile literature.
    [1. Genealogy]   I. Title.
    CS16.G5   929'.1   77–14989
    ISBN 0–531–01455–X

CONTENTS

To Barbara Walker

GENEALOGY

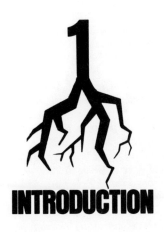

INTRODUCTION

Genealogy, the study of the ancestry of an individual, or a family, is an ancient science, or art, depending on the people involved in the search for their ancestry. In the past it was primarily the wealthy and especially those who laid claim to royal blood—kings, princes, barons, and the like—who eagerly sought out their ancestry. It was important for them, often essential for them, to establish their rights to land, titles, and thrones by way of direct inheritance. When, as happened often enough, genealogical charts provided more than one claimant to titles, lands, and especially thrones, pitched battles, wars, or just plain murder, settled the claims of all parties.

Today, there are still numbers of people, in the United States as well as in other parts of the world, who explore their genealogies in an effort to discover someone of royal blood among their ancestors. But there are many more, particularly in the United States, perhaps because of the recent revival of interest in ethnic backgrounds, who are avidly turning to the science of genealogy to find and become better acquainted with their own roots, humble though they may be.

It is the purpose of this book to help such people in their search by indicating routines for fruitful research into their pasts, sources that are rich with essential and necessary data, methods for collecting and noting such data, as well as ways

Colony of MASSACHUSETTS-BAY, 1776.

WE the Subscribers, Do each of us severally for ourselves, profess, testify and declare, before GOD and the World, that we verily believe that the War, Resistance and Opposition in which the United American Colonies are now engaged, against the Fleets and Armies of Great-Britain, is on the Part of the said Colonies, just and necessary. And we do hereby severally promise, covenant and engage, to and with every Person of this Colony, who has or shall subscribe this Declaration, or another of the same Tenor and Words, that we will not, during the said War, directly or indirectly, in any Ways, aid, abet or assist, any of the Naval or Land Forces of the King of Great-Britain, or any employ'd by him; or supply them with any Kind of Provisions, Military or Naval Stores, or hold any Correspondence with, or communicate any Intelligence to any of the Officers, Soldiers or Mariners belonging to the said Army or Navy, or inlist, or procure any others to inlist into the Land or Sea-Service of Great-Britain, or take up or bear Arms against this or either of the United Colonies, or undertake to pilot any of the Vessels belonging to the said Navy, or in any other Way aid or assist them: But on the contrary, according to our best Power and Abilities, will defend by Arms, the United American Colonies, and every Part thereof, against every hostile Attempt of the Fleets and Armies in the Service of Great-Britain, or any of them, according to the Requirements and Directions of the Laws of this Colony that now are, or may hereafter be provided, for the Regulation of the Militia thereof.

The 38 Names Inrolled on the back of this are of the Town of Tyringham

John Chadwick
Amos Mansfield
Giles Jackson
Joseph Bird
Joseph Allen
Elijah Warrin
Joshua Warrin
Samuel Whedock
Rufus Allen
Ezekiel Hewitt
Nathan Hale
Daniel Markham
Asa Allen
Thomas Colton
Thomas Danford
David Orton

Benja Warren
William Hale
Abijah Merrill
Stephen Taylor
William Bentle
David Black
David Pellett
Ebenezr Chadwick
Isaac Gearfield junr
Consider Hall
John Hale
Benja Markham
Daniel Markham
Parker Underwood
Isaac Gearfield
Amos Northrup

Noah Mather
Wm Morgan
Matthew Jonton
Samuel Graves
Benjr Cross
David Brewer

for avoiding error and confusion in both their research and the tabulation of this research.

A careful reading of these pages plus a diligent application of time and energy on the part of the reader should result in at least a most satisfactory beginning to the discovery of the reader's ancestors and roots.

Old documents may give you clues to your ancestors. This one includes the names of 38 patriots from the Colony of Massachusett's-Bay who agreed to defend the United American Colonies against the British.

A LOOK INTO THE PAST

Since perhaps the beginning of time, ancestors and ancestry have held a special interest for human beings. In fact, in almost every prehistoric culture and in almost every part of the world, humans have worshiped their ancestors as gods or demigods. Even to this day, in Japan and, despite official disapproval, in China, the adoration, if not worship, of ancestors continues.

Primitive peoples worshiped animals as their ancestors— the cow, the pig, the kangaroo, among others, depending on the area of the globe in which they lived. More sophisticated peoples worshiped their gods and goddesses as ancestors. Among the heroes and heroines of Homer's *Odyssey*, Odysseus was said to be the son of Sisyphus; Achilles the son of the sea goddess Thetis; the beautiful Helen of Troy the daughter of the greatest of the Greek gods, Zeus. Remus and Romulus, the legendary founders of the city of Rome, were reputed to be the twin sons of the Roman god of war, Mars.

On the island of Cyprus, the Phoenician kings claimed the mythical Adonis for their ancestor. The kings of Crete were believed to be the sons of Zeus. The conquering Alexander the Great also claimed Zeus as his ancestor. Julius Caesar claimed the goddess of love, Venus, as a progenitor.

The list is almost endless.

The emperor of Japan is still proclaimed to be the reincarnation of the Japanese sun goddess. Hon Xiu-quon, who led a rebellion against the Manchu rulers of China in the middle of the last century, declared himself the brother of Jesus Christ and the son of God. In Muslim countries, to this very day, those who claim descent from the prophet Mohammed are treated with great respect, if not adoration, and are granted considerable political as well as religious power. The late Haile Selassie, the deposed emperor of Ethiopia, claimed he was a direct descendant of the biblical King Solomon and the beautiful Queen of Sheba.

The Bible, itself, is replete with genealogical detail. The ancient Hebrews attached much importance to the "family tree" and, until it was recorded in the Holy Book, passed on orally the stories of their lineage from generation to generation. Whole sections of the Scriptures are devoted to the naming of wives and sons, and the sons of sons, as well as the proposed inheritance of each of them.

The gospel of Saint Matthew begins, "The book of genealogy of Jesus Christ, the son of David, the son of Abraham."

It goes on to name the descendants of Abraham, fourteen in all, to David; then fourteen more generations that culminate in the forced exodus of the Israelites to Babylon; then fourteen more generations to Jesus.

Nor were the Hebrew children averse to claiming a kinship with God.

In Psalm 2, presumably it was King David who sang, "The Lord hath said unto me, 'Thou art my son; this day have I begotten thee.' "

Kings of comparatively more recent times made no claims to kinship with the Creator. Louis XIV of France, who reigned from the middle of the seventeenth century into the eighteenth century, was called the Sun-King, a title that undoubtedly bestowed on him some ancient relationship to the gods, but most monarchs were somewhat more modest. They claimed no direct relationship to the Almighty, or the lesser gods, but ruled by "divine right," with complete power of life and death over all who peopled their kingdoms. And death was often the gift they granted to any who dared to challenge their divine claims to the throne.

In America we don't depend on our genealogies to battle divine rights, for thrones or baronies or dukedoms. At worst, in unhappy circumstances, we bring our genealogies into the courtrooms to contest a will, to dispute an inheritance. But there are those among us who do tend to boast, and not without due pride on occasion, of illustrious antecedents. Many would be delighted to find the name of one of their ancestors among the lineage records published by the National Society of Mayflower Descendants, or the National Society of the Sons of the American Revolution, or the National Society of the Daughters of the American Revolution, or the Society of Cincinnati, founded by the officers of the American Revolution, with George Washington as its first president.

If you can trace your lineage back to Davy Crockett of Alamo fame, or to Mike Fink, the legendary keelboatman of the Mississippi and Ohio rivers, you might be able to consider an even more distant ancestry.

Davy Crockett was in the habit of proclaiming himself "half horse, half alligator, a little touched with the snapping turtle."

Similarly, the ornery Mike Fink would boast, "I'm half wild horse and half cockeyed alligator and the rest of me is crooked snags and red-hot snapping turtle." Shades of primitive worship of animals as their progenitors!

Most of us, however, almost 250 million Americans, have

If you found this document among your family's records, you would know that one of your ancestors had served in the American Army during the Revolutionary War.

[6]

BY HIS EXCELLENCY

GEORGE WASHINGTON, Esq;

General and Commander in Chief of the Forces of the United States of America.

THESE are to CERTIFY that the Bearer hereof *Brister Baker Soldier* in the *Second Connecticut* Regiment, having faithfully ſerved the United States *from April 8th 1777 to June 9th 1783* —— and being inliſted for the War only, is hereby DISCHARGED from the American Army.

GIVEN at HEAD-QUARTERS the *8th June 1783*

G Washington

By HIS EXCELLENCY'S
    Command,

J Trumbull Secty

REGISTERED in the Books
    of the Regiment,

G Curtiss Adjutant,

THE above *Baker*

has been honored with the BADGE of MERIT for *Six* Years faithful Service. *H Swift Col:*

HEAD-QUARTERS, June *10th* 1783.

THE within CERTIFICATE ſhall not avail the Bearer as a Diſcharge, until the Ratification of the definitive Treaty of Peace; previous to which Time, and until Proclamation thereof ſhall be made, He is to be conſidered as being on Furlough.

GEORGE WASHINGTON.

OMNIA PROBATE

'73 FROM '74.

THE PLEASURE OF YOUR COMPANY IS
REQUESTED AT THE FAREWELL HOP
GIVEN TO THE GRADUATING CLASS
BY THE CLASS OF '74.

FLOOR
MANAGERS

| J HANSELL FRENCH | LUTHER R. HARE | WILLIS WITTICH. |

Committee.

J. HANSELL FRENCH	C.E. SCOTT WOOD	WILLIS WITTICH.
WM H. WHEELER	EDGAR B. ROBERTSON	JAS. L. WILSON.
LOUIS A CRAIG	LOTUS NILES	LUTHER R. HARE .

forebears who did not arrive in this New World until long after Davy Crockett and Mike Fink were gone. Most of us will have to travel to Europe, Asia, and Africa to go back more than 140 years into our ancestry.

Only recently, that was precisely what one courageous and determined individual did. Alex Haley, with only the most tenuous of clues, spent twelve years at the task of finding his roots; and he found them. The first of his family in America was a slave by the name of Kunta Kinte. Kunta Kinte, like so many hundreds of thousands of other black people of Africa, had been ambushed and captured by a band of unconscionable slavetraders. He had been fastened in chains and hurled into the ugly bowels of a filthy slave ship. He had been brought to these shores and sold on the block to some Southern slave master. All this had happened to Kunta Kinte some two hundred years ago.

Mr. Haley's genealogical search was a remarkable feat. He accomplished something that had never been accomplished before. For the first time a twentieth-century black man had traced the line of his family back to its very beginning in the New World, to its first American ancestor.

But Mr. Haley was not satisfied with this accomplishment. He ventured further. He discovered that Kunta Kinte, his first American ancestor, had come from Gambia in West Africa, and it was to Gambia that Mr. Haley traveled to explore further his family's origins.

It would not be easy to duplicate Mr. Haley's feat. Nor would it be any easier for certain black Americans to trace their

An old graduation party announcement
may include the names of people
who can give you more information
about your family's roots.

ancestry back to some of the most illustrious characters in America's history. Thomas Jefferson, Alexander Hamilton, Patrick Henry, Daniel Boone, among many other of the most highly respected American explorers, trailblazers, philosophers, political leaders, are known to have fathered black children. To trace one's heritage back to these black children would be undoubtedly a difficult task. But it is not completely an impossible task.

It may prove more difficult, as will be developed, for the descendants of the great waves of immigrants that peopled our land to reach nearly that far back, some two hundred years, into the story of their ancestry. You will have to dig up court records, town records, church records, property records, hospital records, military records, fraternity records, bank records, perhaps prison records, too, among others. You will have to discover naturalization papers, wedding certificates, birth certificates, settlement certificates, among others. It will be essential for you to read through shipping lists, census lists, bibliographies, newspaper and magazine articles—and more.

But all of this will come later, perhaps much later, in your probing for your roots, and this volume will provide you with ways and means of locating all this invaluable data.

Your first steps in your search for your ancestry, however, are comparatively simple. A good detective, in the effort to resolve some mystery, begins with the most immediate clues at hand. This is how you should begin, and your most immediate clues are all to be discovered in your immediate surroundings, within the walls of your own home.

FIRST STEPS

First, provide yourself with the mechanical tools you will need for the task you are assuming:

Pens and pencils,
A notebook or two, to begin with,
A sheaf of paper, size 8½ by 11 inches,
A dozen or more manila folders (to hold your papers),
A box that is large enough to hold the files of paper you will accumulate (actually, a file box).

Your next step is to prepare yourself for your first inquiry, your first efforts at discovering your roots. The results of this initial inquiry will depend on how well you have prepared yourself for it.

Your mother and your father, of course, are your closest antecedents. They can provide you with the most immediate knowledge of the family tree you wish to develop. In the beginning, approach one at a time, and separately. Later you may want to put certain questions to them, when they are both together, to develop certain areas in your discovery, or to verify them. At first, until the family becomes accustomed to questioning, the person-to-person approach will prove more fruitful.

List the questions you will ask your mother and father. Each interview, as you will see, will require a differing set of questions. You begin not by asking their knowledge of the distant past in the family's history (When did our people first come to America?), but by inquiring into the most recent past:

When were you born?

Where were you born?

What was your father's name? How did he spell it? Where was he born? When?

What was your mother's maiden name? How did she spell it? Where was she born? When?

Were you born at home? What was the address of that home?

Were you born in a hospital? What was the name and address of that hospital?

What are the names of your brothers and sisters? When were they born and where?

What church did you attend? Where and when?

What were the schools you attended? What were their names and addresses?

Did you have any special friends at school? What are their names? Do you know what they are doing now (marriage, jobs, careers, accomplishments, etc.)?

What are the names of your aunts, uncles, cousins? Where do they live now? What do they do for a living? Is there anything special one might know about them?

What was your father's work? Where did he work? Did his work take him to different towns and cities? Where?

What was your grandfather's name? How did he spell it? When was he born? Where?

What kind of work did your grandfather do? Where did he work?

What was your grandmother's maiden name? How did she spell it? Where was she born? When?

Did anyone in your family serve in the United States armed forces? When and where?

Let us pause for a moment to say that you should not ask all these questions in one sitting. Long interviews of this nature tend to tire the person questioned and don't make for the best or most accurate results. Spread this series of questions, and the others to follow, over as long a period as you think necessary.

Other questions, to be asked of your mother:

When did you first meet Father? Where?

How did Father court you? Did he take you to the movies, dances, hayrides, etc.?

When did you become engaged? Who was at your engagement party?

Did you have a job before you were married? What did you do?

When and where were you married? Who attended the ceremony, the reception?

Is there anything special about any of the people who attended the engagement and wedding parties (people of note or interesting character)?

Where did you live when you got married?

Did you continue working after you were married?

Where else have you lived since your marriage?

You may ask your father, when you have him alone, most of the above questions. You may ask him other questions, relating to his work and perhaps to his travels.

Were you ever an apprentice? For what kind of work? To whom (spell his name)? Where? And for how long?

Who were your friends at work? How do they spell their names? What are these old friends of yours doing now?

If your father discloses that he moved from city to city, or from area to area, you might ask what occasioned such moves. You might ask your mother the same question.

If any of your grandparents were immigrants, new arrivals

in this country, you might ask from where they came, with whom they stayed on their arrival, and what work they had.

With all these answers, you will have a notebook full of notes.

The next step is to sort out these notes and file them properly.

You might group these notes—one group for your mother, another for your father, and one for each of your four grandparents. Put these groups in folders properly labeled, "Father," "Mother," "Mother's Father," "Father's Mother," and so on.

As to relatives and friends, you may use separate folders as well, or inclusive ones. If you use an inclusive folder, say for your mother's cousins, it would be advisable to list the names included on the outside of the folder. That way, you may more easily find names and addresses you might want to use in your future research.

Three notes:

First, after you have accumulated all this data from your mother and father, and properly filed it, you may profitably call for a joint interview with your parents. This joint interview serves two purposes. For one, it will help clarify any contradictory information you have taken in the separate interviews. For another, reviewing this information may recall names, places, and events that your mother or father had temporarily forgotten.

Make note of this additional information, as well as clarification, and place the information in the proper files.

Second, with your parents, who by this time have become interested, if not involved, in your genealogical project, explore

If your grandparents were immigrants, as these people were, try to find out where they came from, when they arrived, and why they left their homeland.

their knowledge of *their* grandparents. The line of your questioning should follow the questions listed above. The answers will add to your files and develop your research into your roots one step further.

Third, the repeated request for the spelling of names might require some explanation.

People whose surname is Smith or Smyth or Smythe may be complete strangers, or they may be blood relations. If they are related, it is important for the genealogist to have that fact.

Among many families, the closest of relatives go by almost completely different names.

Through the nineteenth century, immigrants coming from the small towns in Europe often had no surnames. They assumed surnames, or had them given to them by immigration officers. As a result, brothers and sisters, arriving in this country at different times, carried different names. One might be called Johnson, another Brown, a third one Jones.

Others shortened their names, or anglicized them. Rubenstein became Rubins, Constantinopolis became Constant; Gutmann became Goodman, Schoor became Shores, Neilsen became Nelson. Sugarman, Sugar, Sager, might very well have all been the offspring of a Zuckerman; and there may well have been another brother or sister who used a name utterly different from the others.

If a person is of African ancestry, there may be even greater difficulty with names. Slaves and their children were generally given the surnames of their masters. But slaves were sold from

Party invitations, award certificates,
and report cards stored away in
the attic provide a record of your
forebears' daily lives, as well as
variations in spelling the family name.

[17]

master to master. Children born on the plantation of the new master were given the surname of that new slaveholder, and not that of their brothers and sisters. Considering the nature of that slave trade, sisters and brothers of the one family might have as many as three, four, or more surnames.

Nevertheless, here too, as elsewhere, the spelling of names is important for identification of kin, and for tracking down the cities, towns, plantations, and farms on which your forebears lived and worked.

Once you have collected all the data you have requested in your interviews with your mother and father, you may have enough material for your first genealogical chart.

Actually there is probably much more pertinent material for your genealogical research right in your own home, and we will come to that in the next chapter. Still, it will be rewarding to draw up the initial, if temporary, chart for your family tree.

You may find it simpler, at some time later in your research, to buy a chart form. Charts may take a variety of shapes, and you may want to write to the Everton Publishers in Logan, Utah, for their catalog of charts. Goodspeeds Book Shop at 18 Beacon Street in Boston, Massachusetts, will send you a book catalog for thirty-five cents (the price may have gone up with inflation). Charles E. Tuttle Co. in Rutland, Vermont, will send you a book catalog free.

But right now, let us indicate a very simple chart that you may use for your initial investigations.

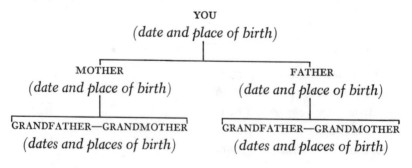

The chart above is a horizontal chart. You might prefer (for aesthetic reasons) a vertical chart:

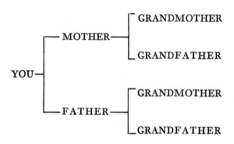

In each of the two charts above you have begun with "You" and fanned out. You might begin with your grandparents and close the fan down to "You," in the following manner:

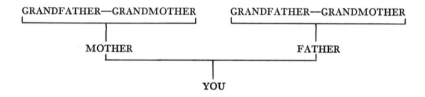

All these charts are quite simple. They do not list your mother's brothers and sisters, nor your father's siblings, nor your own brothers and sisters. You will want these listed as your research progresses. You will discover that every name in your charts will either fill in a blank in your family tree, or lead you into further research for that family tree, or both.

You will also wish to provide more data for each individual on your genealogical chart, as you uncover each new item of information. In addition to time and place of birth, you will want to note the following items: cities lived in, important facts relating to life and work, marriage date, date of death.

This initial chart is very elementary, but it is an important first step that satisfies the need to know that your initial steps in this genealogical search have produced something of a concrete nature. In fact, as your work goes on, you will find it necessary to produce a number of charts: one for your father's side of the family; one for your mother's side of the family; one for the maternal side of your maternal grandmother's family tree; and so on.

But you are a long way from this particular task. You have more searching to do, at this moment, and it may be much and very gratifying searching, within those very same walls of your own house.

ON HOME GROUND

If you search diligently, you will discover a mountain of material for your genealogical files and charts right in the house you live in. The more carefully you search, in bureau drawers, in closets, in bookshelves, in your garages and attics, the more you will find.

Specifically, here is a list of items you should look for:

Photo albums, boxes of snapshots, old framed pictures that have been stored away;

Old diaries, wedding books, baby books, scrapbooks, old letters, newspaper clippings, and perhaps a guest book;

Birth certificates, marriage certificates, graduation diplomas, baptismal and confirmation certificates;

Wedding announcements, birth announcements, death announcements, anniversary announcements;

Any kind of legal paper: wills, deeds, mortgages, leases, contracts, tax notices;

Citizenship papers, visas, passports, perhaps alien registration papers;

Any kind of material relating to the family's finances: bankbooks, bills, receipts, old account ledgers;

Old driver's licenses, fishing and hunting licenses, business licenses;

Old schoolbooks, school prizes, school pictures, report cards, yearbooks;

Any papers or cards that reveal membership in some fraternal organization or sorority, or affiliation with a church, community organization, or political party;

Military records, awards, separations, and pensions;

Souvenirs of some trip, some party, some gala occasion;

Old toys, and other memorabilia, which for one reason or another have been stored in the attic;

The family Bible.

With some of the material you discover at home you will be able to verify certain facts you have already obtained from your parents: primarily births, weddings, and deaths.

For most of this material, however, you will need the aid of your mother or father to fully utilize your findings for your genealogical project.

Your father and mother may not be able to identify every item you discover, but whatever they do identify will help you develop a fuller and richer genealogical chart. The pictures, diaries, certificates, and other things will undoubtedly revive old memories for your parents, bring up new names and new places, new events; and your genealogical files will expand enormously.

In developing this new material, however, you must, as always in this project, be well prepared to ask the proper questions, and take the proper notes.

Let us say, for example, that you have discovered an old photograph album. Do not race immediately to your mother or father with a flood of questions about it. Better, pore over the album. Note the unfamiliar faces. Prepare a list of questions you will ask about each of them.

An award certificate such as this one will tell you where and when a distant relative attended school.

Mrs. Sylvanus Reed's School

Ruby C. Simmons

Having attained for eight Months

The Highest Mark

for Conduct, and in her English Studies

receives this expression of the loving approbation of

her faithful friend

New-York, June 1st 1888   Caroline S. Reed

What is (or was) this person's name? How do you spell it?

How well did you know this person? What kind of person was he or she? What did this person do for a living?

Where did he or she live?

What was this person's family like?

Just how is this person related to us?

Did he or she ever do anything that was particularly exciting or interesting?

At an appropriate time, you will discover that your mother (or father) is as interested in these pictures as you are. Of course the details you will get in answer to your questions may not always be pertinent to your research. Picture albums often contain chance snapshots of forgotten acquaintances. But, often enough, a picture will recall some forgotten hero or heroine in the family, a poet, a trailblazer, an adventurer; and sometimes a scamp.

"This is a picture of your grandfather's cousin. He was a Rough Rider with Teddy Roosevelt."

"This is your great-aunt Emma. She went overseas as a nurse in World War One."

"I can't remember his name. Your grandmother would remember it. If I'm right, he went west during the gold rush. I don't know whether we ever heard of him again."

You write down these responses in your notebook. Later, you transcribe your notes on an 8½-by-11-inch sheet of paper and put them into their proper files; or, more likely, start a new file for each new name.

What you get from your parents, and the photo album, are additional people who belong on your family tree. What you must do is follow the new leads—learn what you can of the Rough Rider, your great-aunt Emma, and the member of the family who was apparently lost in the gold rush. Following these leads should help you discover still other members of your family, as well as some interesting stories they may develop for your family history. We will indicate how you may follow up these leads in another chapter of this book.

You may use the method you employed in exploring the potential in the photo album again for any other pictures you find around the house: the box of snapshots, framed pictures, school pictures, school yearbooks, wedding pictures, and the like.

Old certificates, legal papers, licenses, scrapbooks, membership cards, souvenirs, diaries, and old letters should provide you with more names, more stories, more leads. Again, they will bring to mind names, people, and places your parents have temporarily forgotten.

For each name and place you will press your parents, gently of course, for as much detail as they can give you.

If they tell you that your great-uncle George was a sailor, ask what ships he sailed, what kind of ships, the ports his ships visited, his job as a sailor, and what he is doing now, if he is still alive. If they haven't all the information you want, ask them who has more information about great-uncle George.

If they say that your great-aunt Alice went west with her husband, ask her husband's name, why they went west, where they settled. If great-aunt Alice was among the homesteaders who peopled the west, what did she grow on her farm, did she ever return east, how many children did she have, and where are those children now? Again, if they can't answer all your questions, ask who might.

Detail. Detail. Detail is necessary if you want to write as complete a genealogical history as possible.

Old toys, old silverware, the odd old plate, newspaper clip-

Over: a carefully posed picture such as this may have marked a special event. With luck, someone in the family will remember the details and names of the people involved.

[25]

tate, and such portion shall enure to the said Albert T. Patrick.

Eleventh: I give, devise and bequeath to Albert T. Patrick, formerly of Texas, now of New York, all the rest and residue of my estate, real, personal and mixed, heretofore or hereafter acquired and wheresoever situated.

IN TESTIMONY WHEREOF, I, the said William M. Rice, to this my Last Will and Testament, have subscribed my name and affixed my seal in the presence of *Morris Meyers and David L. Short* as subscribing witnesses, who sign the same as subscribing witnesses at my request, in my presence and in the presence of each other this 30th day of *June*, A. D. nineteen hundred (1900).

W M Rice (Seal)

Signed, sealed, published and declared by the said William M. Rice, as, for and to be his last Will and Testament, in our presence, and we, at his request and in his presence and in the presence of each other, have hereunto signed our names as witnesses this 30th day of *June* A. D. nineteen hundred (1900).

Name.	Occupation.	Address.
Morris Meyers	*Lawyer*	*168 Henry St Manhattan, N.Y.*
David L. Short	*Publisher*	*404 Bradford St Brooklyn N.Y.*

pings with perhaps no more than birth or death notices, an old service uniform tucked away in mothballs—all should lead, with proper questioning, to more names for your files, more names to follow up in your research.

For your parents, old toys should revive memories of childhood, old neighborhoods, and young and old friends. Old silverware, and old heirlooms, will recall the people who passed these things on to your parents.

The newspaper clippings will bring back to your parents events they had forgotten.

If the old service uniform belongs to your father, ask him where he served, under which officers, perhaps in what battles and what wars. He will probably recall some of his comrades-in-arms. And all this is invaluable to your project.

Poring over old bills, receipts, and account ledgers should provide you with much material on how your grandfathers and grandmothers, great-grandfathers and great-grandmothers lived, how they earned their money, how they spent it, their necessities for living, and how they indulged in luxuries.

Deeds and mortgages should tell you where your antecedents lived, in what areas of the country, whether city, town, or farm.

Old wills should offer you a host of names, who inherited what from whom. After examining these old documents, in addition to asking your parents about these new names, you might well ask about the stories behind the wills.

Where did the testator live? How did he or she accumulate the estate? Why did he or she apportion the wealth that particular way? Were there any people left out in the will, and why?

Finally, and certainly one of the most important finds you

An old will may contain
interesting information
about your family's past.

may be able to make in your own home, there is the family Bible. If you are fortunate, it will be a very old Bible.

It is an ancient custom, still very much in vogue, for families to list all their vital data in a Bible, generally on the pages that separate the Old Testament from the New Testament. If you discover such a Bible, these pages will list the births, baptisms, confirmations, marriages, and deaths of all the immediate members of your family for generations back.

Such a list will serve to confirm, of course, some of the data you already have, and probably provide more that you need to acquire. Perhaps it will introduce a host of names not yet mentioned.

Again, go to your parents for whatever information they may have on these names, or for the names of other members of the family who can help you in this research.

This search in your own home for materials pertinent to your genealogical project will undoubtedly take considerable time, but every moment spent on it should more than adequately reward your efforts.

When the search, and the research with the help of your parents, is done, you should have enough material to begin to draw up a series of more detailed genealogical charts. You might even begin to write a preliminary draft of a genealogical history of your family.

Actually, until you are prepared to draw the one, huge, master genealogical chart for your family, all other charts should be considered preliminary or working charts.

Right now, let us say that you have been able to ascertain certain salient facts, the so-called vital statistics, back to your great-great-grandfather. This will allow you to draw several complete charts and probably a number of incomplete charts.

For example, let us assume that you have all the data related to your father's direct descent from your great-great-grand-

father. Your chart of this direct lineage might well take the form
illustrated below:

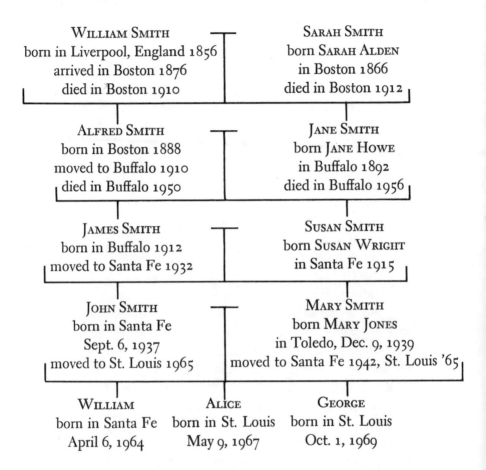

WILLIAM SMITH ——— SARAH SMITH
born in Liverpool, England 1856   born SARAH ALDEN
arrived in Boston 1876   in Boston 1866
died in Boston 1910   died in Boston 1912

ALFRED SMITH ——— JANE SMITH
born in Boston 1888   born JANE HOWE
moved to Buffalo 1910   in Buffalo 1892
died in Buffalo 1950   died in Buffalo 1956

JAMES SMITH ——— SUSAN SMITH
born in Buffalo 1912   born SUSAN WRIGHT
moved to Santa Fe 1932   in Santa Fe 1915

JOHN SMITH ——— MARY SMITH
born in Santa Fe   born MARY JONES
Sept. 6, 1937   in Toledo, Dec. 9, 1939
moved to St. Louis 1965   moved to Santa Fe 1942, St. Louis '65

WILLIAM   ALICE   GEORGE
born in Santa Fe   born in St. Louis   born in St. Louis
April 6, 1964   May 9, 1967   Oct. 1, 1969

You will note a number of obvious genealogical omissions
in the chart above. For example, it is likely that the original
William Smith had more than one child, that you had several
great-great-uncles and aunts. They have all been omitted. There
may be two reasons for such omission. For one, the size of the
paper you have at hand does not allow for a fuller chart. Second,
you haven't sufficient data for a fuller chart.

Let us say that you do have the necessary information. Then the genealogical chart, beginning with your great-great-grandfather, would start in the following manner (for the sake of space, we will limit the chart to names, without any other data):

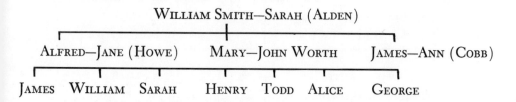

WILLIAM SMITH—SARAH (ALDEN)

ALFRED—JANE (HOWE)   MARY—JOHN WORTH   JAMES—ANN (COBB)

JAMES   WILLIAM   SARAH   HENRY   TODD   ALICE   GEORGE

Again we have shortened the chart. We have yet to list the people James, William, Sarah, Henry, Todd, Alice, and George married (all part of your family tree), as well as their children and grandchildren.

Once more, it may be the lack of space or the lack of complete detail that is responsible. But this is no great fault. On the contrary, it would be wiser for you to make separate charts for each of the children of William and Sarah Smith, and the progeny that followed. First, it will be easier for you to check your progress with the genealogy of each branch of your family. Second, with individual and smaller charts, you will more easily make corrections of errors, as well as supplement the data already recorded.

The number of such smaller charts will be quite large, but also very rewarding.

Such charts must include the genealogical lines of those on the maternal side of your family.

For example, according to the chart on page 31, you know that Alfred Smith was the son of William and Sarah Smith. You should create a chart for Alfred Smith's wife, Jane Howe Smith. The chart tells us only that Jane's father went by the name of Howe. What was his first name? Where was he born? When? When did he die? What was Jane's mother's name? It is quite possible that Jane (Howe) Smith's parents were in America long before her father-in-law, William Smith, arrived in Boston. There was a British general by the name of Howe? Does he belong in your family tree?

What about the family of Susan Wright Smith, the woman who is your grandmother? What is her lineage?

And your mother, Mary Jones Smith? How far back can you trace her family?

So far we have discussed the possibilities involved in creating genealogical charts of your immediate family. Think of the possible heroes (and villains) you may find by drawing the genealogical charts for all your other relatives, from your great-great-uncles and aunts, and whom they married, to the present day.

There will be time to collate all these smaller and individual charts into one great genealogical chart when you have amassed all the data you possibly can for the genealogical history of your family.

Similarly, if you wish to write a history of your family, it might be better to postpone such an activity until all the facts have been accumulated. Still, you might enjoy starting such a project, even if all you could write would prove to be scarcely more than a skeleton outline for such a story.

The story you might write would read something as follows:

"My great-grandfather, Heinrich Vogel was born in Hamburg, Germany, in 1864. He was a tall and good-looking young man, and a hard worker. He worked as an apprentice for a printer by the name of Hans Wolff. Hans Wolff was so impressed with my great-grandfather that he allowed his daughter, the pretty Hannah, to marry my great-grandfather.

"Heinrich Vogel and his wife came to America in 1890, riding steerage on the ocean liner, *Deutschland*. They landed on Ellis Island, where they were met by Heinrich's cousin, Johann.

Johann was a printer, too. He had a little shop in Bayonne, New Jersey. That is where he took my great-grandfather and great-grandmother to live with him and his family, and to work with him.

"In 1894 my grandfather was born in Bayonne, and was christened Wilhelm Vogel. Later, my grandfather changed his name to William Bird. This was an anglicizing of his German name. I think he did this during the First World War, when the United States was at war with Germany. In any case, he enlisted in the American army, became a staff sergeant, and fought in the Battle of Château-Thierry, where he was wounded. Fortunately, the wound was superficial. What was more important, as it developed, was that he met and became friendly with Sergeant Roger Turner. Sergeant Turner had a small machine shop in Bridgeport, Connecticut, and asked my grandfather to join him in a partnership after the war. This partnership, which my grandfather accepted, worked well for a long time.

"It was in Bridgeport that my grandfather met and married Amy Stokes. Amy Stokes' father was a lawyer in Bridgeport who said that his own grandparents had come from Norway to find themselves a home and farmland in Wisconsin. (He didn't know when he had dropped his Norwegian name for an American name.) Amy Stokes' mother, as my grandmother tells it, was a Lee from Virginia, and she was certain, though she could not prove it, that she was a descendant of Lighthorse Harry Lee, one of the legendary generals of the American army in the Revolutionary War.

"Grandma Amy was a little woman, but she made up for her size with her enormous energy. She thought Grandfather could do better for himself if he had his own business, and she persuaded him to move to Akron, Ohio, where he opened up his own small toolshop.

"It was in Akron, in 1942, that my father was born. . . ."

Obviously this is a threadbare story. It not only leaves out much detail in the personal lives of these people, but it also suggests that the author of this story ought to check on his grandmother's tales, particularly her claim to being a descendant of Lighthorse Harry Lee.

Still, it is an example of what might be considered an outline for a much fuller and richer story of a perhaps interesting family.

But, we are considerably ahead of the intentions of this book. There is still a major job of research to be done. You may have done a thorough job of exploring all the sources of information you could find in your own home for your genealogy, but there are many more sources for such information to be discovered, and means and ways for reaching and tapping those sources.

Let us proceed.

DIGGING DEEPER

After you have exhausted all the sources for your genealogical project in your own home, your next step is to reach for whatever genealogical information you may be able to get from your nearest relatives: aunts, uncles, grandparents, cousins.

Your procedures in this phase of your genealogical research will be much the same as those you used investigating the sources in your own home. The material you will discover in the houses of your relatives will be similar to what you have discovered before: photographs, albums, souvenirs, old letters, and so on. The questions you will ask your relatives will be much like the questions you asked your own parents.

But come prepared with that list of questions:

When and where were you born?
What was your mother's name? How did she spell it?

If you came across a photo such as this in one of your relative's old albums, you could be pretty sure that someone in your family had gone off to the goldfields.

What kind of work did your grandfather do? Where? What church did your family attend? And so on.

Be sure to have your notebook with you and to write down all the information you receive as accurately as possible.

These visits to your relatives will serve two purposes. One, they will help to verify data you have already collected. Two, they will probably provide you with additional details, as well as a number of new faces, new names, new locations, new stories, and new leads to follow.

Verifying data, it should be said at once, is a most important function in developing a genealogical story. You must be sure of your facts, sure of your data. If details, as to the spelling of names, dates of birth, journeys, business deals, property holdings, and so forth, are not identical as you receive them from different relatives, you'll have to put on your detective's hat and run down all your evidence until you come as nearly as possible to the "whole truth and nothing but the truth" in your investigations.

To verify certain data you have collected, you may have to consult town records, court records, shipping lists, and such. Later on in this book, you will be given directions on how to approach such sources. But right now, the verification you obtain from your relatives should do.

If some of your relatives live a distance from you, you might turn to letter-writing to get whatever information they may be able to give you. Of course, you must be precise in the manner in which you put your questions, particularly in letter-writing. Questions of a general nature will produce broad and imprecise responses. Specific questions will bring you, most likely, the kind of specific data your genealogical project requires.

Here are samples of two letters you might need to write:

Dear Aunt Martha,

I am working on a genea-logical chart for our family. which I think will interest you. and perhaps you can help me.

I've been told that you received the last letter great-grandfather Burroughs wrote from Texas (before the Alamo). Could you send me a copy of the letter?

By the way. nobody here seems to know the rank he held in the army. If you know, I'd appreciate your letting me know.

DEAR COUSIN FRANK,

AUNT MARY TELLS ME THAT YOU HAVE THE DEED TO THE OLD FAMILY FARM IN KANSAS. COULD YOU SEND ME A COPY OF THAT DEED? I NEED IT FOR THE GENEALOGICAL STUDY I AM DOING OF OUR FAMILY.

IF YOU CANT SEND ME THE DEED, WOULD YOU TELL ME:

THE DATE OF THE DEED

WHO SIGNED THE DEED, AND IN WHAT COUNTY?

WHAT ARE THE DIMENSIONS OF THE FARM?

WHAT IS ITS EXACT LOCATION?

I WOULD ALSO APPRECIATE YOUR TELLING ME, IF YOU CAN, WHEN THE FARM WAS SOLD, AND TO WHOM IT WAS SOLD.

AND, IF YOU HAVE THE INFORMATION AND IT IS NOT TOO MUCH TO ASK, PERHAPS YOU CAN TELL ME WHAT WAS GROWN ON THE FARM AND HOW IT WAS SOLD. PERHAPS YOU CAN FIND SOME OLD LEDGER WITH ALL THAT INFORMATION IN IT.

Notice that in each letter the questions are specific, each question calling for a specific response. And each specific response should add that much more data to your files, and for your family tree.

There are other people, besides relatives, who live nearby and who may be able to verify your accumulation of facts, or add to these facts. There is the local barber, the couple who have owned and run the general store for countless years, the men working in the town garage, the woman who runs the town library, some of the older and retired teachers still living in your town, the pastor or priest of your church, and many others.

Some of these people have known your family for years. This is especially true if you live in a small town or village. Ask precise questions and you will get, most likely, a number of interesting and precise responses.

Of course, as always with your project, you should prepare yourself well for your interviews with these neighbors and friends. You should have all the questions you are going to ask them prepared beforehand.

When did you first meet my father (mother)?

What was the town (village, street) like at that time?

Where did you play? What games did you play?

Were you in the service with my father? What kind of soldier (sailor, marine, etc.) was he?

Do you remember my grandfather (grandmother)?

Did my mother (grandmother) sing in the church choir? Was she a good singer?

Over: a longtime neighbor of your grandparents may remember your mother when she was a little girl—and even have a picture such as this to show you.

What kind of books did my father (mother) read?

Was my father (mother) especially good in any particular subject in school?

The list of possible questions is endless, and the answers to your questions will probably suggest other questions.

"We liked to go fishing," might be the response to one of your inquiries.

It follows that you will ask, "Where did you go fishing? What did you catch?"

Another response might be, "Your grandmother made the most beautiful patchwork quilts."

It follows that you must ask, "Did she win any prizes for her quilts? Where did she show them? Do you know anybody who still has one of her quilts?"

Of course you will not get all this wealth of data in one interview. Most likely you will interview all these sources a number of times. After each interview, there will be three tasks facing you.

First, verify as far as possible, with your parents, and perhaps other relatives, the new information you have gathered.

Second, recopy all the data you have received on those 8½-by-11-inch sheets of paper you have; and file the papers properly.

Third, using your new information, formulate the follow-up questions that have been suggested by your interviews, write them down so you will not forget them, and then follow up.

*The curious thing about this picture
is that some of the people are
wearing traditional clothes and
others are dressed in contemporary
clothes, which might be a clue to when
part of the family arrived in America.*

[45]

BROADEN YOUR RESEARCH

After you have amassed all the information you possibly can for your genealogical story from the things related to you by friends, neighbors, and acquaintances, you will begin to explore other areas and sources for data essential to your family story.

Except for the American Indians, as you well know, all the ancestors of people living in the United States came from foreign lands. Many came from English-speaking countries, but the overwhelming number of immigrants who came to the New World spoke other languages and arrived with a variety of their own customs and practices. These immigrants usually settled in areas where they could meet and live with and speak with those who spoke their native tongues and followed their native ways. They created their "Little Italys," "Little Russias," "Little Athens," "Chinatowns," and so on.

They also organized a number of clubs, associations, fraternal orders, benevolent organizations, and cultural orders,

A certificate of membership in the New York Mechanick Society would indicate that the ancestor to which it belonged had been a skilled manual worker.

[46]

both for mutual protection and to preserve what they could of their old-country ways and manners. Some of these organizations grew, with the great influx of immigrants, and have chapters all over the land. Some remained small fraternities, limiting themselves to those who had emigrated from some particular small town in Austria, Poland, Russia, or elsewhere.

It is quite likely that one or more members of your family joined, or is still enrolled, in one or more of these organizations.

Here is a partial list of the huge number of such organizations that exist in America:

American Sons of Erin
Congress of Russian Americans
Sons of Italy
Ukrainian Dniester Benevolent Society
Roumanian Jewish Federation of America
the various Deutscher (German) Verein
Polish American Congress
Workmen's Circle
Knights of Pythias
Knights of Columbus
Elks
Shriners
Masons
Odd Fellows
Loyal Order of Moose
Prince Hall Grand Lodge
Daughters of the Eastern Star
Alpha Grand Lodge
(*The last three should be of special interest for black people researching their family trees.*)

There are also a number of service organizations: Veterans of World War One, Veterans of Foreign Wars, Jewish Veterans of the U.S.A., and the American Legion, among others.

For those whose forebears were among the earliest American settlers, there are the Society of Mayflower Descendants, the Sons of the American Revolution, and the Daughters of the American Revolution.

From such organizations you may be able to obtain some minimum information, perhaps no more than the dates of membership, offices held, and possible contributions. From others, particularly from the benevolent societies, you may be able to learn the point of origin of some member of your family, the date of his or her death, and the location of the burial site. From such organizations as the Society of Mayflower Descendants and the Daughters of the American Revolution you may be able to obtain, if your family goes back far enough in America, a complete lineage record.

If you have any evidence or believe that any of your family belonged to any of these benevolent, cultural, or patriotic organizations, then certainly you should approach them for whatever information they can give you for your genealogical project. The larger of these organizations probably have branches where you live, or nearby. Visit these chapters, first preparing the questions you want to ask. If you cannot go in person, you should turn again to letter-writing, asking proper and precise questions for precise responses.

You will find the names and addresses of these organizations, if they have branches in or near your community, in your telephone book. They will appear under the listings of "Clubs," "Associations," "Fraternal Societies," "Social Service Organizations," and the like.

You will find the names and national addresses of these organizations and associations in your public library.

If you visit a local branch of a society, it should be enough to say to the officer in charge of records, "I believe my great-grandfather was a charter member of your organization. Could I ask you to check on it?"

If the officer-in-charge discovers your great-grandfather's

name in the rolls, you might then ask, "Can you tell me when he joined the organization?" "Can you tell me when he died and where he was buried?"

Once the officer-in-charge understands that your purpose is the development of a family history, he or she may be able to provide not only the data you asked for, but some other interesting facts about the life and times of your great-grandfather.

If you write to a distant national office of some association, you will need to be more formal, and to list your questions more formally.

The material you gather from these associations, fraternal orders, benevolent societies, and so on will serve primarily to confirm the data you already have. It may, of course, provide you with data missing from your charts and history. It may also give you new leads to follow for your genealogical project.

Even though a number of the smaller fraternal orders, organized to provide mutual aid to recently arrived immigrants from specific localities, no longer exist, the list of such organizations still functioning is fairly extensive. Here are a few:

Croatian Fraternal Union of America
Czechoslovakian American Sokol
Western Bohemian Fraternal Association
Danish Brotherhood of America
Holland Union Benevolent Association
Greek Pancretan Association of America
Hungarian William Penn Fraternal Association
Association of Polish Women in America

A relative's fraternity certificate might lead you to more valuable information from other members of the organization.

Theta Xi Fraternity

Knows with reverence and pride the memory of

Who gave his life in the cause of his country in the Great World War. To his family we present this formal expression of our abiding consolation as the name of our Brother is engraved high on the Roster of the Eternal Chapter of Theta Xi Fraternity.

_____ PRESIDENT

_____ SECRETARY

Dear Sir or Madam:

I am working on a genealogical chart of my family. Would you be good enough to supply me with the following information concerning John T. Applegate:

Date of birth
Date of joining your
    organization
Offices he held, if any
Date of death
Burial site

Very truly yours,

Slovenian Women's Union of America
Swedish Independent Order of Svithiod

If these organizations have branches in your city, you will find their addresses in the phone book. If not, you might consult L. R. Wynar's *Encyclopedic Directory of Ethnic Newspapers* in the local library. A letter to the appropriate newspaper should bring you the address you want.

VISIT YOUR LIBRARY

Libraries, you will discover, are replete with information that will be important in your search for your roots. There is much material of a general nature that you may dig up in the collection of newspapers, magazines, and microfilm usually stored in the larger libraries. The libraries also, generally, have a section devoted to genealogy.

Go to your library prepared. That is, know specifically what you want to try to find there.

Let us say that your great-uncle Tom was in San Francisco at the time of its great earthquake. To perhaps get more information about this great-uncle, you would ask for the microfilm of newspapers on or about the date of the earthquake, and peruse them for whatever data you could find. If you have the exact date and place before you go to the library, you will save yourself and the librarian much time in getting to the material you want.

Let us say that you have reason to believe that one of your ancestors signed our country's Declaration of Independence. You would then be prepared to ask for (or find yourself in the library catalog) books in which the signers of the Declaration are listed. You might also have in mind going through the library catalog to discover whatever material the library may have on the lives of these signers of the Declaration of Independence.

In the genealogical section of your library, most of the material you will discover will be regional in nature: New England, the Northwest, the South, etc. But you will also discover, in this section, papers, pamphlets, articles, and books that are limited to families of one specific state: Virginia, Massachusetts, Utah, and so on. You may even find, particularly in libraries that are exclusively devoted to genealogy, genealogies of single families, one of which may be your own.

The larger the library, of course, the more productive your visits for genealogical material will be. If you live in a small town, however, the small town library may provide you with an abundant amount of material on the life and times of your own family.

For the location of libraries devoted completely to genealogy, which are almost exclusively situated in the larger cities, look up their names and addresses under "libraries," "associations," and "museums" in the yellow pages of your telephone directory.

If your ancestry is black, you might make a special point of looking for Carter Woodson's *Free Negro Owners of Slaves in the United States in 1830*, and *Free Negro Heads of Families in the United States in 1830*. If your local library does not have these books, the librarian may be able to get them for you from an associated library.

RECORDS, OFFICIAL AND UNOFFICIAL

Unofficial records may be considered those you will find in your church, or in the societies to which members of your family belonged. Official records may be considered those you will find in government files—local, town, state, and national.

You should find both types useful for your genealogical studies, for verifying data, supplying missing data, and perhaps generating new leads for your project.

Visit your church or temple, or the one your family used to attend. An official of the church or temple will have records of its congregation, including baptisms, christenings, bar mitzvahs, weddings, and funerals. If you go with a specific request, the pastor or rabbi will undoubtedly make these records available to you.

Specific requests will follow the line of all your other specific requests for information:

When was my great-grandmother Ann Wilson baptized?

When was my great-great-grandfather William Morgan married? What was my great-great-grandmother's maiden name?

In many cases, the records in your church or temple will be limited. Pastors and rabbis do not always have the time or facilities for maintaining detailed records.

Sometimes the very oldest church records may be found in

the state organization of a particular denomination. If your church is part of such an organization, ask your pastor for the address and write to the organization for any specific information you think you need for your family history.

There are also some church and temple historical societies and divinity and rabbinical schools that collect and keep old records of local congregations.

Again, your pastor or rabbi may be able to direct you to a useful source. But be certain, as always, in your letters of request for information, to put your questions directly and ask for specific information.

Town records will provide you with land records (titles, mortgages, claims and sales, boundaries, etc.). They will supply you with probate records (petitions, wills, heirs, court case files, court actions, judgments). They will provide you with marriage records, school board records, poor relief records, registers of voters, and much more, including local history files. Almost nothing of the life of a town is omitted in its records.

The town clerk is generally the person in charge of all such records and, since town records must always be open to the public, you should have no difficulty in having them opened for you. It would be advisable to call or write for an appointment to avoid catching the person in charge in the midst of a hectic day, and unable to give you any personal attention.

Since these records are so voluminous, be certain to be prepared with precise questions about the precise information you wish to obtain.

Over: the Beth Israel Temple in Portland, Oregon, kept photographic as well as written records of its congregation over the years. You might recognize a distant relative when browsing through records of this sort.

If the town whose records you wish to search is some distance from where you live, you might write to the clerk of that town for the information you want. Again, and certainly very important in such an instance, be sure of the spelling of the names of the people about whom you are inquiring, and make your requests as specific as possible.

What is the date of Walter Burns Bogan, Jr.'s birth?

What is the date of the sale of Henry Williams Porter's farm (in the vicinity of Roundtree Stables), and for how much was it sold, and to whom?

It may take a while to get a response from the town clerk to whom you have written. Sometimes, because the records have been destroyed by fire or flood or some other natural disaster, your reply may read, "No record."

Nevertheless, as a good genealogist you have to write such letters and, often enough, the response to such letters may be rich with reward.

State archives and, particularly, federal archives, with their multitudes of records, include a tremendous amount of material that should prove useful to you in the development of your family history.

From the state archives you can receive, in addition to land, probate, and vital records, information on military pensions, jury records, and military records (in some instances from the French and Indian Wars through the conflict in Vietnam) that include everything from casualty lists to battle reports. You can even get registers of prisoners and parole rolls. They will also provide matriculation lists of the state universities, and welfare records.

Most state historical societies print historical journals that might prove invaluable to your research. Any question pertaining to the history of the state will probably bring you a response rich with information.

To get the information you may desire, address your specific inquiries to the proper state committee or bureau or private state historical society. Your own state assemblyman or state senator will give you the names of the persons to address, if you request that information from him or her.

The above procedure is best for obtaining state information since different states assign different departments for similar data. For example, to obtain vital statistics in Iowa, you would need to write to the Curator, Historical Building in Des Moines. In New York, for the same data, you would have to write to the Department of Health in Albany.

From the federal government, in addition to land records and pension records, you can get the national census, taken every year since 1790. (You may also get state census records, taken by different states over the years, from your state capitals.)

To obtain any national census from 1800 to 1880, in microfilm, address the National Archives in Washington, D.C. (The cost changes with the times.) For census records after 1880, address the Bureau of Census, U.S. Department of Commerce.

Among the more interesting items you may get at the National Archives in the nation's capital are payrolls that go back to the days of the American Revolution. The Archives has all kinds of miscellaneous records, including a variety of petitions made by individuals and groups and sent at one time or another to an elected representative in Congress. Perhaps you may find the name of one or more of your ancestors in such lists.

Last, but certainly not least in the importance of your research, you might venture into the cemetery, preferably the oldest cemeteries you can find. Here, you may wander about leisurely, looking for names that are familiar to you, family names, reading the inscriptions on the stones that mark the places where the deceased lie.

Over: old gravestones are another source of information about the past.

To the memory
of Mrs. Betsey
Tracy consort of
Mr. Peleg Tracy, &
daught. of Mr. Jesse
Brown, who died
March 16th. 1792.
aged 10 Years &
8 Months.

Blessed are the dead
that die in the Lord

Some of the stones in the older cemeteries will be broken, the result of many, many years in the rain and snow and wind. Some will have sunk deep into the ground. On some it will be difficult to read the inscriptions because the lettering has been damaged by time and the elements of nature. You must read the words that have been carved into the stone, nevertheless, as best you can: names, dates, relationships (husband, wife, son, daughter, and so on). You must carefully transfer this information to your notebooks. These words may be the final verification you need for the vital statistics in your genealogical pursuit. They may also give you clues for further research in your work.

You may think you have certain discrepancies in your project when you compare what you have discovered in these cemeteries with what you have already written in your notebooks, or have in your files. Names you have already noted may not match those on the gravestones. Dates may not agree.

The explanation for these seeming discrepancies may be quite simple. In the old days people were a trifle careless about spelling. You have only to think of the different spellings for William Shakespeare. O'Ryan may have been spelled O'Ryen; Beaufort, Bofort; Schmidt, Smit; Dunne, Done or Doan or even Downs.

As for dates, for many years there were two calendars in general use throughout the world. There was first the Julian calendar, established by Julius Caesar more than two thousand years ago. In the last years of the sixteenth century, however, it was discovered that the Julian was not an accurate calendar, that it made the calendar year just about thirteen minutes longer than the solar year.

Pope Gregory XIII corrected the error, moving the calendar ten days forward. In other words, if a person's birthday was April 10 by the Julian calendar, it became April 20 by the Gregorian calendar.

Not everyone adopted this correct calendar immediately,

and the difference in days between the two calendars grew greater. When George Washington changed his birthday from February 11 to February 22, there was an eleven-day difference. In the 1900s, that difference became thirteen days.

This difference, of course, might explain away some discrepancies you may have in dates of birth, marriage, death, and so on. Nevertheless, you must check and recheck these dates, as well as the spelling of names. You may be understandably eager to get as far as you can and as fast as you can in your search for your roots, but you must avoid, as much as possible, any kind of error you might make in the process.

There will be a discussion of other areas in which errors may be made, and how to avoid them, in the last chapter of this book.

MIGRATIONS

To locate some particular member, or a whole branch, of your family (to complete your genealogical chart), you may need to recall the story of migrations to America.

For example, you must know, in the beginning:

the English settled on the Atlantic seaboard;
the Dutch in New York;
the Germans in Pennsylvania, Maryland, Ohio;
the French Huguenots largely in South Carolina;
the Welsh and Irish along the Atlantic coast;
later, the Scandinavians in the Midwest;
the huge number of immigrants from Eastern Europe
principally in the larger cities of the East.

You must also consider the mass migrations that took place within the continental United States, and into Canada. For example, there was the mass movement west when the federal government opened that region to land grants; the mass movement of people to the Pacific areas during the gold rush; the numbers of people loyal to King George III who fled to Canada during and after the American Revolution; the blacks who fled from slavery to find freedom in Canada; the massive migration, particularly of black people, from the South to the industrial and urban centers of the North, during and after World War II.

To refresh your memory and to explore migrations to and from specific areas in the country, you may study any number of articles, pamphlets, and books (most likely available at your library) on the subject.

For example, there is:

History of the Huguenot Emigration to America
by Charles W. Baird;

The Yankee Exodus
by Stewart H. Holbrook;

The Westward Flow of Southern Colonies before 1861
by William W. Lynch;

Migrations from Connecticut after 1800
by Lois M. Rosenberry.

Consult the catalog in the library for your own special needs. The librarian will try to help you find whatever it is you wish to find.

To locate information about your first American ancestors who arrived in the New World by ship, you may consult the National Archives in Washington, or write to them for the information you desire. Of course, if you write, you must have considerable information on hand: names, dates, and perhaps names of ships as well.

If you visit the Archives, you will discover that it will provide not only entire passenger lists of the ships that brought

Over: the S.S. Pennland *was one of the ships that carried many immigrants to America in the late nineteenth century.*

immigrants into the United States (after 1820), but the age, occupation, point of embarkation, and port of arrival of each passenger. For immigrants who arrived after 1919, you will have to consult the records of the Department of Immigration and Naturalization, also located in Washington, D.C.

Naturalization papers, incidentally, should prove of great assistance in locating important data on your distant forebears. These papers contain the name, age, and place of birth of the person naturalized, as well as the place (and date) from which the person emigrated and proof of residence, and also the name (and date) of his or her point of arrival.

You may be able to get the data on such naturalization papers from the county clerk's offices, presuming you know the county in which the naturalization was granted, and *if* this naturalization was granted before September 27, 1906.

For naturalization papers after that date, you will need to get in touch with the office of the Commissioner of Immigration and Naturalization in Washington.

Obviously, your efforts in this direction may produce very significant results.

10

CONFUSION AND CLARIFICATION

Dates on gravestones, in the listings you may find in family Bibles, or in other documents may confuse you momentarily but, as soon as you become aware of the differences between the Julian and Gregorian calendars, you should be able to clear up the confusion.

There are other areas, however, where the confusion is not so easily clarified, and where you may very well make serious errors. The first and perhaps most significant of these errors may come in the area of names.

We have mentioned the way names in families have been spelled in a variety of ways, and have even been changed in the course of years. For example, a name like Pierce may be found to be spelled Pearce or Piers or even Perse. Or you may discover that the original name of the family, Piccolomini, has been changed to Pico or Pick or Pike, or even to Colon. While it is not simple, you can trace these variations on a name back to its original form. But, as you may learn if you do not already know, there are many people, completely unrelated, who carry the same surname. And it is here that you may make a huge mistake while tracking down your genealogy.

There are so many Smiths, so many Browns, Greens, Johnsons, Cohens, Murphys. You could make quite a list of such names: Rossis, Wongs, Nielsens, and so on. But there are less common names, too, that families without any blood ties at all carry in common.

Obviously, it is quite easy to make an error unwittingly in this area of your research. You can avoid that error, as you must, by refusing to seize hastily upon a name as proof of family relationship. You must check and recheck your data for links that connect that particular name with your family history. You must make certain that the name you have discovered, however familiar, was carried by a person who truly belongs to your family tree.

Another source of error, particularly when your search carries you back a hundred years and more, is the failure to understand some of the family nomenclature used at that time; that is, the way they used such words as "cousin," "brother," "sister," even "father" and "mother."

We still speak of our "sisters and brothers" in a religious congregation, referring to people who are not related to us by blood. But, in any kind of document that might be developed today, you would be certain to make plain the difference between brother or sister and "brother or sister in religion." This difference, you will discover, was often omitted in documents of the past.

"Cousin," even today, in a legal sense means "next of kin." Almost universally, however, cousin today is the name we give to the children of our aunts and uncles. This was not so in the past. In old wills and other documents, cousin might mean nephew, niece, grandson, granddaughter, or anyone who was not specifically a son or daughter in the family. Similarly, a father-in-law was termed "father," a mother-in-law "mother."

"Mistress" or "Mrs." may also lead to a bit of confusion. Today "Mrs." is a title given to a married woman, though now a number of married and unmarried women prefer the title "Ms." At one time, however, "Mistress" and the abbreviated "Mrs." were titles given to any woman who was the head of a household, whether she was married or not. It was a title that was given to any woman who was an owner of slaves. Even the governess in a household, a rich household of course, who took care of the education of the children of her employers, was called "Mistress." Also, the word "Mistress" was once just a polite form with which to address any woman at all.

You must be careful in your research with this nomenclature, as you must be careful with all the data you uncover. You must check and recheck, particularly in those areas where errors are most easily made.

Finally, you must know that there are no shortcuts in this search for your roots. There may be any number of people around who will offer to furnish you with a family "coat of arms," a family tree, or both. You read their advertisements in newspapers and magazines. You even get their offers in the mail. But be very wary of such advertisements and such offers.

There are very few American families who possess genuine coats of arms, mostly dating back to the British and French. Those you may purchase through the mails are likely to lack authenticity, and are often pure frauds.

Family trees that come to you from organizations that make a business of providing genealogies are rarely, if ever, thorough and satisfactory. Generally, these people will provide you with a few words on the origin of your surname, information about a scattering of famous people who carried the name, and a rather questionable record of the first families in America with that name.

How surnames originated always makes for interesting reading, of course. But there are many families with the same surname, and you will receive no proof that the famous people mentioned, or those "first families in America," were in any way related to you. More often, if not always, the money you have spent for the information you receive is utterly wasted; and you may be sure that you will receive no information at all from these genealogical business people until you have paid them a required fee.

There are, however, a number of genuine and respected genealogists. You can find their names in their announcements and advertisements in respected genealogical journals, brochures, and magazines. These are the people to consult, if you think they can help you in your genealogical search. You can find these genealogical journals, pamphlets, and magazines, in the larger city libraries and, especially, in the libraries that devote themselves completely to matters of genealogical study.

Still, and this is important to know, even the trained and respected genealogists will not be able to help you unless you can provide them with some good genealogical data. You must supply them with a number of names and places and dates, all accurate, all checked and rechecked, before they can carry your studies further. This data, these names and places and dates, you must find yourself.

If you are truly interested in discovering your genealogical past, you must become a detective. You must look for clues and follow them all, including the least promising of them, to wherever they may lead. You must become an investigative reporter, searching out sources, checking and rechecking whatever information you may dig up.

Dig is the word.

You must dig, dig hard and deep and wide, if you earnestly want to discover your roots. If you are truly earnest about this venture, patient and persevering, then all your digging, for however long it may take you, will be well rewarded.

BIBLIOGRAPHY

Allaben, Frank, and Washburn, Mabel. *How to Trace and Record Your Own Ancestry.* New York: The National History Co., 1932.

Bennett, Lerone, Jr. *Before the Mayflower.* Chicago: Johnson, 1964.

Corsi, Edward. *In the Shadow of Liberty.* New York: Arno, 1969.

Doane, Gilbert H. *Searching for Your Ancestors.* Minneapolis: University of Minnesota Press, 1960.

Everton, George B. *How Book for Genealogists.* Logan, Utah: Deseret, 1973.

Frazer, Sir James G. *The Golden Bough.* New York: Criterion, 1947.

Haley, Alex. *Roots.* New York: Doubleday, 1976.

Hamm, William A. *From Colony to World Power.* Lexington, Mass.: Heath, 1962.

Hansen, Marcus L. *The Atlantic Migration.* New York: Peter Smith, 1961.

Jacobus, Donald L. *Genealogy as Pastime and Profession.* Baltimore: Genealogical Publications, 1968.

Jones, Vincent L.; Eakle, Arlene H.; Christensen, Mildred H. *Family History for Fun and Profit.* Provo, Utah: Community Press for The Genealogical Institute, 1972.

Morrison, S. E., and Commager, H. S. *The Growth of the American Republic.* New York: Oxford University Press, 1960.

Williams, Ethel W. *Know Your Ancestors.* Rutland, Vermont: Tuttle, 1961.

INDEX

Relatives, interviews with, 36, 38

Rosenberry, Lois M., 67

Roumanian Jewish Federation of America, 48

School board records, 57

Settlement certificates, 10

Service organizations, 48

Shipping lists, 10

Shriners, 48

Slavery, 9, 17–18

Slovenian Women's Union of America, 53

Society of Cincinnati, 6

Society of Mayflower Descendants, 6, 49

Sons of the American Revolution, 6, 49

Sons of Italy, 48

Spelling of names, 17, 18, 60, 64, 65, 71

State archives, 60

State historical societies, 60–61

Surnames. *See* Names

Swedish Independent Order of Svithiod, 53

Temple records, 56–57

Town clerk, 57, 60

Town records, 10, 57, 60

Ukranian Dniester Benevolent Society, 48

Unofficial records, 56–57

Verifying data, 38, 45, 72, 73

Veterans of Foreign Wars, 48

Veterans of World War One, 48

Washington, George, 6, 65

Wedding certificates, 10

Welfare records, 60

Western Bohemian Fraternal Association, 50

Westward Flow of Southern Colonies before 1861, The (Lynch), 67

Woodson, Carter, 55

Workmen's Circle, 48

Wynar, L. R., 53

Yankee Exodus, The (Holbrook), 67

ABOUT THE AUTHOR

Henry Gilfond, a free-lance writer, has taught in New York City junior high schools, edited literary and dance magazines, written for radio and television, and done reviews for the *New York Times Book Review*. He is the author of two plays, as well as a number of books and short stories. He lives in New York City with his wife Edythe, a costume designer.